IMAGES OF ENGLAND

TUNSTALL
REVISITED

IMAGES OF ENGLAND

TUNSTALL
REVISITED

DON HENSHALL

TEMPUS

Frontispiece: A view of the Market Square in the 1950s, by now
called Tower Square, shows that the clock at the top of the building
has been replaced by ornamental ironworks. Apparently, the weight
of the stonework above the clock had begun to bear down and
threatened to destroy it. William Durose was commissioned to
replace it and created a shape which resembles a Star of David. This
design was used as it was a very efficient shape which helped to
spread the load evenly around the circle.

First published 2006

Tempus Publishing Limited
The Mill, Brimscombe Port,
Stroud, Gloucestershire, GL5 2QG
www.tempus-publishing.com

British Library Cataloguing in Publication Data.
A catalogue record for this book is available from the British Library.

ISBN 0 7524 4143 4

Typesetting and origination by Tempus Publishing Limited.
Printed in Great Britain.

Contents

	Acknowledgements	6
	Introduction	7
one	Tower Square and the Arnold Bennett Connection	9
two	High Street and Station Road	17
three	Education	33
four	Work …	41
five	Rest …	69
six	… and Pray	91
seven	People	113
eight	Tunstall's Neighbours	121

Acknowledgements

I am grateful to the many people who responded so favourably to my first book on Tunstall. They have provided me with additional information and material which, together with my own collection, has enabled this second volume to come to fruition so soon.

In particular, I would like to thank the following: David and Margaret Mycock of Abacus Bookshop, Milton; John Abberley, of *The Sentinel* and *The Way We Were*; The Arnold Bennett Society; Sid and Brenda Bailey; Leonard Barber and Brian Barber; Members of The Churches Together in Tunstall, especially parishioners of the Sacred Heart Catholic church including Shelia Broad, Alf and Marie Cole, Mark Meaney, George and Marion Owen and Maureen Rafferty; Bill Davies; Tom Deakin; Barbara Gregory, Lord Mayor's secretary, City of Stoke-on-Trent; Dorothy Jones, Joan Wallbanks and Captain Liz Elmer, of the Tunstall Corps of the Salvation Army; Members of the Potteries Postcard Society; Katey Goodwin of the Potteries Museum & Art Gallery; John and Sue Richardson; Roger Simmons; Elaine Sutton; the management of Tunstall Assurance … and all those who have helped, encouraged and inspired me in any way to be able to share this book with you now. I especially thank my family for their continued patience and belief in me.

I remain indebted to those who, over the years, have painstakingly researched the many documents and recorded facts about Tunstall and the surrounding areas which have thus created reference books for the benefit of past, present and future generations.

Introduction

Tunstall Revisited takes a further illustrated look at the social history of this important town.

The Six Towns of Tunstall, Burslem, Hanley, Stoke, Fenton and Longton, were combined as a Federation in 1910 and subsequently united to become the City of Stoke-on-Trent in 1925. Each town has a very distinct character and, despite the downturn in manufacturing industry over the past twenty or so years in the city, the people seem to remain loyal to their roots. Whilst there is mobility within the towns it would still be rather unusual for there to be mobility between them.

Past generations were able to find all that they needed in their respective towns – education, employment, religion, leisure, health care, etc, and they were practically autonomous mini-cities.

Federation and the later City status only served to centralise the administration of each town. Each one retained its own shopping area with some chainstores duplicated in each town. Major manufacturers had branches across the city. Whole families could, and did, work together on the potbanks which were virtually at the end of the street where they lived. There was little need to move out of the area in which they grew up. Nowadays, with the loss of industry and the creation of new housing developments, a small degree of mobility is beginning to occur.

In my first book, *Tunstall*, I gave a glimpse of life in the town over the past 150 years or so and showed some of the elements which have helped generations of families to form this town. The reaction to that book was phenomenal and I am grateful to the many people who not only bought copies for themselves but also for their relatives and friends across the globe. I have been able to share the success by giving illustrated talks across the city to various groups of people and the reaction when a long-forgotten friend or relative is recognised on the screen has been quite moving.

I hope that *Tunstall Revisited* will produce a similar reaction for the reader and I feel especially privileged to share these images of yesteryear with you.

Don Henshall
2006

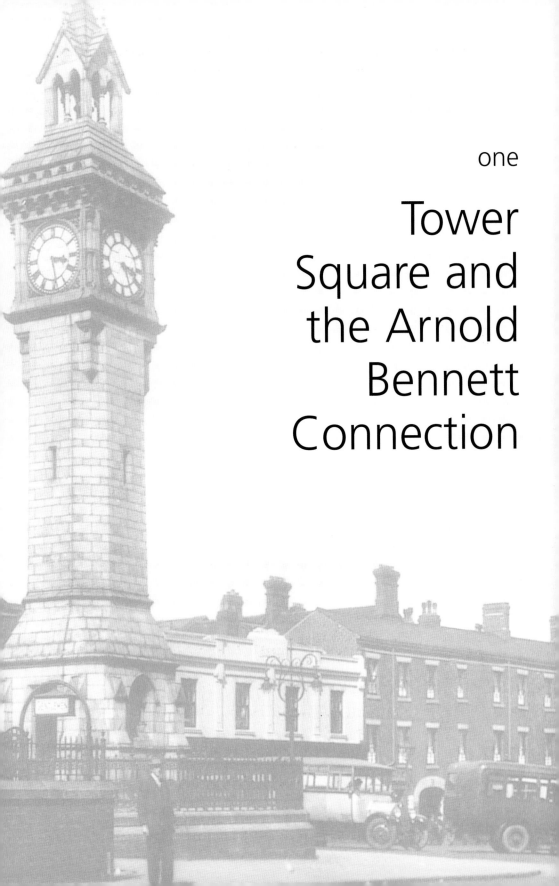

one

Tower Square and the Arnold Bennett Connection

Tower Square is one of the oldest parts of the town. Many of the buildings which line the Square date back to the mid-1800s. Mostly they are simple two-storey buildings which would have housed the shopkeeper's family on the upper floor. The exception lies in the north-western corner of the Square. The building on the corner of Forster Street has an extra storey and is quite prominent because of its size. It has housed many different kinds of business over the past years and is currently a tool shop.

Arnold Bennett (1867 – 1931) is a local author of note. His prolific works provide his readers with an immense variety of topics and he is much underrated. His writings are intelligent, witty, funny, poignant and sometimes sad. His stories of life in the Five Towns (Bennett deliberately omitted Fenton) are a wonderful mirror of social history in the late nineteenth and early twentieth centuries. One of his most famous works is the trilogy *Clayhanger*. The middle book is *Hilda Lessways*, published in 1911 and has a direct link with Tunstall – or Turnhill, as Bennett calls it. He changed all the local placenames but they are all easily recognisable as his descriptions of the area were so accurate. *Clayhanger* was made into a successful television series in 1976. Another of Bennett's popular books, *The Card*, was filmed in, and around, Burslem, in 1952 and starred Alec Guinness and Glynis Johns. This was later re-written as a musical comedy and played to London audiences in 1973 and 1999.

Hilda Lessways' story is set in 1878. The prominent clock tower was not erected in the Square until 1893 and its site was previously occupied by the original Town Hall (see below right). The following extracts from Bennett's novel give an insight into his wonderful ability to paint atmospheric pictures in the reader's minds. I commend his work to you.

The Market Square of Turnhill was very large for the size of the town. The diminutive Town Hall, which in reality was nothing but a watch-house, seemed to be a mere incident on its irregular expanse, to which the two-storey shops and dwellings made a low border...Still, to the east of the Square, across the High Street, a vast space was being cleared of hovels for the erection of a new Town Hall daringly magnificent... and she went straight into Dayson's little fancy shop, which was full of counter and cardboard boxes and Miss Dayson, and stayed therein for at least five minutes, emerging with a miraculously achieved leisureliness. A few doors away was a somewhat new building, of three storeys – the highest in the Square. The ground floor was an ironmongery: it comprised also a side entrance, of which the door was always open.

Upstairs was the solicitors' office where Hilda first meets George Cannon – but you really need to read the rest for yourselves!

Arnold Enoch Bennett, 27 May 1867–26 March 1931. Having grown up in Hanley and Burslem, Bennett left the Potteries in March 1889. He spent much of the rest of his life living in and around London except for a period of approximately ten years (1902 – 1912) when he lived in Paris.

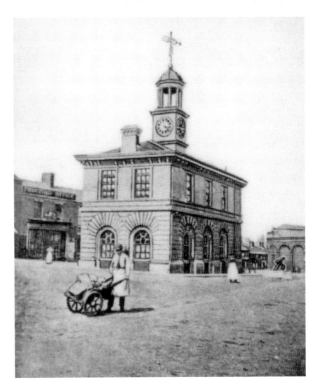

The Old Town Hall, *c.* 1873. (*Bygone Tunstall*, William J. Harper)

TUNSTALL, CLOCK TOWER.

Market Square, with Arnold Bennett's character George Cannon's tall office building to the right,
c. 1910. This building had another claim to fame in the early 1980s when it was used as a rent-collector's

office in the television series *The Sharp End*, starring Gwen Taylor. A lot of the location filming was done in and around Tunstall, though the series was supposedly set in Lancashire.

An early view of a practically deserted Market Square, *c.* 1900. At the top of the Square is the building which, according to its date-stone in the front gable, began life in 1821. From 1823 to 1851 it served as the original Mount Tabor Chapel of the New Connexion Circuit in Tunstall. To the right of the clock tower can be seen the roofs of the nearby Jubilee Chapel and Schoolrooms.

Above: A view from around 1925 taken from the pavement outside the Oddfellow's Arms where, according to the lamp outside the building, Parkers' Fine Ales were available inside. Five buses are lined up in the Square and, remarkably, they are all different makes, models and companies! Between the two buses at the rear can be seen the arched entrance leading to the stables and yard of the original Sneyd Arms Hotel.

Opposite above: This drawing shows the Sneyd Arms Hotel around 1910. The stables and loose boxes were to the left of the archway and were later converted to a garage prior to 1916.

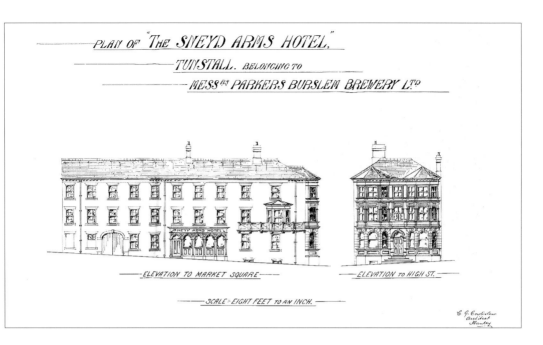

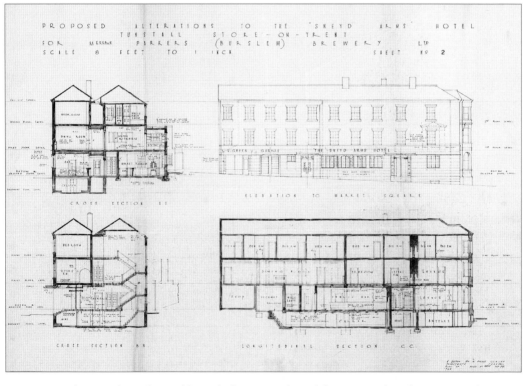

By March 1919, plans submitted by Parker's Brewery showed the garage to have been converted to a lock-up shop (A. Greer) and in 1937 further plans were approved for the archway to lead to a covered garage in the old yard at the rear of the hotel. Subsequent plans drawn in 1939 and 1949 proposed that, after major reconstruction, the archway would become what is now the main entrance to the Hotel.

Above: A clearer view of the Sneyd Arms archway and adjacent shop can be seen in this view taken from the upper floor of the Town Hall, *c.* 1930.

Left: This clock tower is not the one in Tunstall, Tower Square; it is actually in Barnstaple in Devon. This one pre-dates Tunstall's by thirty-one years being erected in 1862. Barnstaple's clock tower was designed by R.D. Gould and it is believed that the Tunstall design was adapted from the original plans, with minor modifications around the base to accommodate the bust of Sir Smith Child in whose memory the tower was erected.

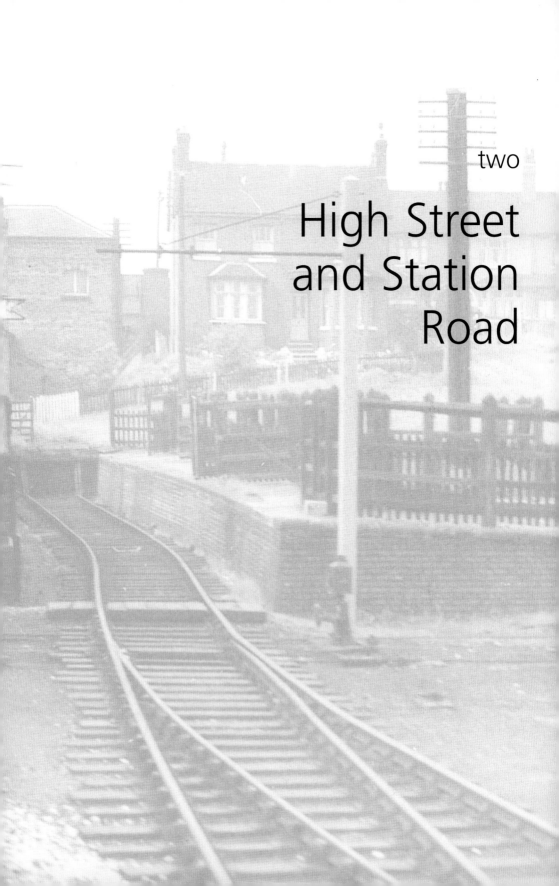

two

High Street and Station Road

This early postcard shows a view around 1910. It was published locally by T.H. Pemberton and sent by visitors to their uncle and aunt in Burnley in 1913. The message on the reverse states that they are 'Having a ripping time, been in the Potteries and Steel Forges watching the manufacturing processes'. Who said that factory tours were a modern innovation? This couple were enjoying their factory tours some ninety-three years ago! The shop on the right is Leonard Piggin's Chemist shop on the corner of Rathbone Street. On the left, the road being crossed by the boy in the foreground is Smith Street, which no longer exists. The shops between here and John Street (later Farndale Street) in the distance were demolished and the area redeveloped in the 1960s. The shop on the left with all the goods hanging outside is Beesley & Co., which seems to have had a short life in the first decade of the twentieth century.

John Johnson and Son are obviously very proud to promote their new hearse and funeral cars on this advertising postcard. The business officially traded from Madeley Street, but its premises extended to the High Street where this picture is taken. For over eighty years, the business has enjoyed an enviable reputation with generations of bereaved families in the locality and is still in existence today (though no longer a family concern). Tunstall can boast another long-established firm of funeral directors in Clement McGough and Sons, which has also been in existence for approximately eighty years.

Prior to 1920, Pattyson's ran their grocers shop on the corner of High Street and Madeley Street (next door to John Johnson and Sons, the undertakers). In this early photograph we can see Mr Charles Pattyson and his assistant posing at the entrance to the shop, whilst an errand boy sits in the delivery cart ready to go on his rounds.

According to Kelly's Directory for 1896, Mr Henry Smallman ran a confectionery shop at 113 High Street. In the Kelly's Directories for 1921 and 1928 there is mention of a Mrs Sophia Smallman running a grocery business from 104 High Street. The style of this horse-drawn van would suggest an age that is more likely to link with the earlier date than the later one.

Above: The Wheatsheaf Hotel is pictured here around 1910. The licensee was Mr Arthur Rigby and he appears to have had a long association with the premises. The pub is still a popular drinking establishment today and looks much the same as in this view. Several alterations to the interior have taken place over the years – probably the most significant being the conversion of the stables at the rear to a garage.

Above: Two of Beresford, Caddy & Pemberton's AEC Flatbed lorries pictured in the 1930s.

Right: In 1933 Holdridge's Restaurant offered 'Hot Luncheons Daily 12 to 2.30; Teas and Light Refreshments'.

Opposite below: In 1865 the firm of Beresford, Caddy & Pemberton began trading as transport contractors. Their boast was 'Haulage of any description – to any extent – with our extensive Horse Vehicles of all kinds'. As the business grew, lorries replaced horses. The above picture shows two examples of the vehicle fleet in 1936/7. The little three-wheeled van was a new innovation, being manufactured by Reliant after the designer, Tom Williams, left Raleigh, which had developed the prototype. This van was powered by a 700cc engine and was state of the art in its day. On the side of the Beresford van it states 'Express Parcels Service'. On the passenger door it offers a delivery service to Southport, St Helens, Birkenhead and Wallasey. Beresford Transport, as the business eventually became known, became one of the best known fleets in the country. It was scaled down in the 1990s, by which time it was running international services and was eventually purchased by R.G. Bassett & Sons, of Tittensor, in April 1996, after a long and illustrious history.

'Private Parties, Weddings and Dinners' were catered for in their 'Spacious Dining Hall Lounge and Coffee Room'. At their peak, Holdridge's had branches in Longport and Wolstanton.

Above: In the early 1900s, indoor hockey on roller skates was a favourite sport in North Staffordshire and Tunstall had its first purpose-built rink in 1909 on a site behind the first Barber's Palace.

Opposite above: Since 1900, after moving to Goldenhill with his wife and two children, George Barber had been giving Lantern Lecture shows around various parts of the locality. He became a pioneer of cinematograph, known then as Living Pictures and shows were given at Sunday schools, Town Halls and Lecture Halls. However, the cinematograph process was dangerous and presented a safety risk. Consequently, an Act of Parliament was introduced in 1909 and George Barber decided to construct his first, purpose-built cinema. This is a view of the first Barber's Picture Palace in Tunstall at that time.

This fine body of men is the 1910/11 Championship Team from Tunstall's Station Road Rink. The rink manager at the time was George Temperley. However, the venture was short-lived and the premises were purchased by George Barber in 1911 who tried to keep the business going for another twelve months.

POST CARD

PALACE, TUNSTALL.

∴ Don't miss our ..
New Super SERIAL

Commencing next Monday, August 20th.

Considered to be the Finest Serial ever produced.
∴   ∴   In 15 Episodes.   ∴   ∴

Featuring - Miss CLEO MADISON

Above: This postcard is advertising a fifteen-part serial at the Picture Palace, Tunstall. On the reverse side is a picture of the star, Miss Cleo Madison.

Right: Cleo Madison was an American actress who appeared in almost 100 films. She also directed seventeen, produced four and wrote two films. Her career began in the theatre in 1910 and she moved into films soon after. In 1914 she appeared in her first serial for Universal Pictures. Following a nervous breakdown in 1922, due to her heavy workload, Miss Madison was out of work until 1924 when she returned to make several more films. She suddenly left the business some time later and died in California in 1964.

Opposite above: Eventually, George Barber decided to close the rink and he rebuilt his Picture Palace on the combined site.

Opposite below: The Picture Palace was rebuilt again in an art deco style and this picture shows it in its heyday in 1937. Many people today can still recall with fondness their visits to Barber's Palace in Tunstall. Sadly the cinema closed in the 1980s and was demolished some time later.

George Herbert Barber was born in 1860. He was a character (what Arnold Bennett would call 'a Card') and became a legend in his own lifetime. His accomplishments were phenomenal and he is remembered with much affection by generations of Tunstall families. He rose from very humble beginnings to become Lord Mayor of the City of Stoke-on-Trent in 1929-30 and he brought pleasure to thousands of people who were entertained at his Picture Palaces. George Barber was a pioneer who introduced the silent movies and then the talkies to Tunstall. But for a sad quirk of fate George would have been the first cinema proprietor to show talking films in North Staffordshire. He was brought up in the Methodist tradition and later preached in the Tunstall and other circuits. He became an active member of Stoke-on-Trent Council in 1910 as well as a member of the Board of Guardians. During his term of office as Lord Mayor, Alderman Barber met members of the royal family and foreign delegates who were attracted to the city by the grand Wedgwood Bicentennial Celebrations. He was also in attendance during the Mass held on 27 June 1930 to celebrate the opening of the Sacred Heart church in Tunstall.

In 1922, George Barber was one of the first to take advantage of Government subsidies on flights from Manchester to London and he became a regular user of aeroplanes. In 1931 he undertook a tour of Europe by plane and the following year he flew to Palestine and Egypt. George had hoped to fly to Russia in 1933 but was unable to do so because of a restriction on visas. He was, however, able to travel by sea and embarked on this trip on 29 July of that year. George Barber's tales of his extensive travels have been documented in a book that he published himself in 1934 called *Small Beginnings*. In 1937 he published a further biography entitled *From Workhouse to Lord Mayor*. Each of these is a fascinating read and they are highly recommended if copies can be traced. Alderman Barber is remembered for his broad Potteries' accent and for not attempting to deny his roots no matter in whose company he found himself. There are many anecdotes of his which have become part of local folklore and these demand their own documentation in a separate publication. George Herbert Barber died in 1946, aged 86. His grandson Leonard followed in George's footsteps to become Lord Mayor of Stoke-on-Trent in the year 1952-53.

A train passes through what appears to be a deserted Tunstall station on Saturday 31 May 1958.

The Tunstall Benevolent Burial Society was established in 1839. This was a truly innovative way of allowing the general working classes to be able to afford a decent burial. Up to that time, poorer people had to rely on the generosity of relatives and friends for help to bury their dead. The Society had the vision to offer a sum to be paid at death in return for a maximum payment of one halfpenny a week, and the key was to have a number of collectors who travelled around the district visiting families at home on pay-day. The business was run on what is known as the Mutual system and all profits belonged to the members of the Society. Many obstacles were overcome, particularly in the early days, but perseverance paid off as, one hundred years later, in 1939, the Society had grown to be the largest collecting society in England and the sixth largest in Great Britain.

The Society Rules were registered on 9 April 1840 and they contained the following poem:

> And art thou dead? dear infant art thou dead?
> No mother's tears can raise thy fallen head,
> Peace to thy spotless shade; in quiet rest.
> Why should I weep, since thou are ever blest?
> Nature demands the tribute of a tear,
> And decent rites shall grace thy humble bier:
> Our plans afford relief unto the poor,
> For which we need not beg from door to door.

Here are officers and committee members of the Society on an outing to Rudyard in 1896. The officers elected on 3 March 1893 were: president, James Beech; vice president, Charles Cope; secretary, Peter H. Bloor; treasurer, David Reid. The Management Committee consisted of: James Podmore, James Addison, John Garner, Henry Cope, Thomas Rhodes, William Beech, Aaron Parr, William Hind, Charles Hewitt, Hamlet Hopkins, Arthur B. Cooper, William Heath. The offices were at 52 High Street.

In November 1909, premises known then as Stanley Hall, in Station Road were purchased. Mr A.R. Wood was appointed as architect to prepare plans for the redesigning of the building. Station Chambers were officially opened in October 1910.

Three past presidents: Charles Hewitt, vice president 1898-1904 and president 1905-1908. Thomas Goodwin, vice president 1905-1908 and president 1909-1927. George Baker, vice president 1909-1927 and president 1927-?.

Due to changes in Government legislation the Society was obliged to change its name on 1 January 1924 to the 'Tunstall and District Assurance Collecting Society'. By 1928 the Society had experienced rapid growth in business and from 1910 it had grown five times larger. It needed to expand its offices and was able to acquire additional space in an adjoining building. New plans were drawn up and the refurbished building was opened on 21 March 1929.

Above, left and right: At the time of the Society's centenary, in 1939, the main officers were: John W. Hulme (committee 1898; trustee 1918; vice president 1927; president 1928). Joseph Cope (chief clerk 1912; assistant secretary 1921; secretary 1922).

The Management Committee, November 1939. Back row, left to right: David Evans, Leonard Callaghan, George Baker, Harry Pemberton, Myles McGough. Second row: James Davies, John Cooney, Frederick Pickerill, Harry W. McBrine, Ralph Riley, Luke McDonald (all committee members). Front: Arthur Shaw (trustee), William Rhodes (trustee), John W. Hulme (president), Joseph Cope (secretary), William P. McGough (trustee).

Opposite below: Officers, Management Committee and staff, November 1939.

Joseph Cope, secretary, seated at his desk in 1939. The Society continued to grow and expand and has been a support to countless families in Tunstall and beyond for well over 160 years. The business is a credit to those early pioneers who saw the need and responded to it, and to their successors. Tunstall Assurance became part of the Order of Foresters Friendly Society Ltd on 1 January 2004.

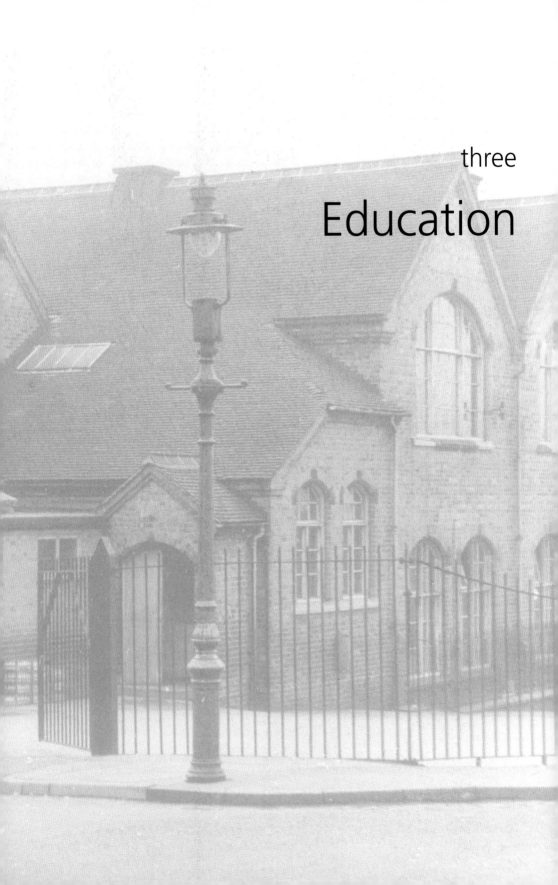

three

Education

Above: The High Street Secondary School is in the background as the Salvation Army Band led a procession to the opening of Brownhills High School for Girls in 1929.

Left: This view shows the grand entrance hall at Brownhills.

Opposite above: Everyone looks hard at work in the new and impressive school library.

Opposite below: Tunstall RC Junior and Infants was built in Oldcourt Street, on the corner of Roundwell Street in 1902-3. In earlier times it served also as a secondary school, until the Blessed William Southerne RC Secondary was opened on Little Chell Lane in 1957. A new Catholic Primary school was opened on Queens Avenue in 1990 to serve the needs of Tunstall, Burslem and Fegg Hayes parishes. This school was dedicated to St Wilfrid following the closure of Cotton College, which, until the 1980s, had been an exclusively boys' boarding school in the Staffordshire Moorlands. Tunstall RC was closed and subsequently demolished.

BROWNHILLS HIGH SCHOOL, STOKE-ON-TRENT. The Library.

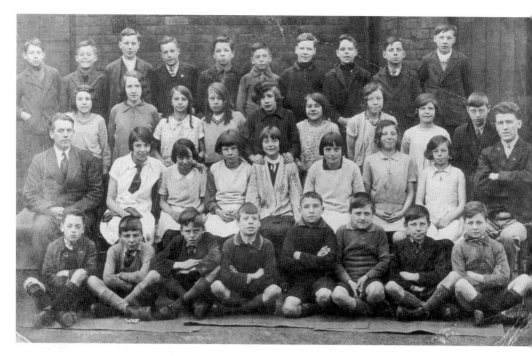

A Tunstall RC class photograph, 1930s.

A winning team! This picture shows the victorious 1954 football team. Mr Broad sits on the left and Mr P. O'Reilly (Headmaster) is to the right.

Right: In this Tunstall RC staff photograph, Mr O'Reilly sits in the centre of the front row, while, to his left is seated Nellie Keane, and to his right is Eileen O'Reilly. Standing at the back, from left to right are Gerard McCormack, Jim Broad, Alf Gillaker and Paddy McNamara.

Below: Summerbank County Secondary Girls' School opened in 1909 and it is obvious from the following pictures that their pupils enjoyed their performing arts. The first picture shows the cast of *Quality Street* in 1943/44.

Above: Around the same time the school also produced *Children in Uniform*. This will no doubt bring back some memories for the girls taking part.

As well as Catholic schools in Tunstall there was also an Anglican presence in the field of education. St Mary's church was built in 1859 to serve as a Chapel of Ease in the south of the town. Christ Church continued as the parish church and served the north. In 1862, a schoolroom was built on the south side of St Mary's. After many years of service to the Anglican community in Tunstall, the school closed when a new primary school was opened in 1971. The school buildings subsequently found new life as a staff restaurant and function room for the nearby H. & R. Johnson Tile company. The church remained until around 1980, after which both school and church were demolished.

Opposite below: Up on Bankey Fields could be found Joby's Pond, which was an ideal spot for pond-dipping, as these girls from Summerbank found out, *c.* 1960. The class was led by the Biology teacher Miss Brinkworth and, by all accounts, no one fell in!

Stanfield County Technical School finally moved into its new premises on High Lane in 1960. Since 1949 the new site had slowly been transforming into a new purpose-built school but, when all the pupils were finally on one site, having vacated the Moorland Road school in July of that year, parts of the 'new' school were already some eleven years old!

Every old boy will immediately spot the flaws in this picture; the pristine aprons, absence of swarf on the benches and floor; everyone working in unison on the same filing stroke! You can almost hear the soft piped classical music in the background. If only it had been like that!

four

Work …

Work in Tunstall has taken many forms over the centuries, but the prime industry has been based around the manufacture of pottery since the fourteenth century. By 1750 much growth had taken place and once the main road through the town became a turnpike in 1763 and the Trent and Mersey Canal became operational in 1777, development grew at a swift pace. Other industries sprang up around this core in a complimentary way and many of these are depicted in this chapter. Much pioneering work took place in Tunstall over the next hundred years as new techniques were developed with mixtures of clays from other areas and fluid glazes were developed. By 1900 there were nineteen large pottery firms operating in Tunstall manufacturing earthenware, china and vitrified ware. Many of these firms were run by generations of the same family so it was not unusual for whole families of workers to be employed in them. Sons followed fathers and daughters followed mothers into a variety of skilled and unskilled occupations.

This picture shows packers hard at work, c. 1875. Finished ware was packed in crates and barrels which were stuffed with wood wool and straw to prevent breakages. Not every firm had its own crate makers department, so several little ancillary industries came into being, making the containers and selling them on to a variety of local manufacturers.

A CHINA WAREHOUSE.

Eager customers are awaiting the receipt of their orders and here we see several ladies working in a Glost Warehouse in 1875 packing the individual requirements. Soon the containers would be loaded onto a cart for their onward journey.

This is a typical view of a potbank in Tunstall — but which one? There are no identifying marks on the buildings but the bottle ovens and the huge chimney are quite distinctive and should not prove too difficult to trace.

Beneath its surface, apart from a proliferation of clay, Tunstall also had an abundance of coal and ironstone. As a consequence, numerous primitive, small-scale mines emerged in and around the town in the seventeenth and early eighteenth centuries. Access to these materials, particularly for the manufacture of pottery, enabled the fast expansion of the industry in the eighteenth and nineteenth centuries and while the potbanks became larger the mines also needed to develop in more efficient ways. Many of the mineral workings around Burslem and Tunstall were owned by Hugh Henshall Williamson of Greenway Bank and after the opening of the Biddulph Valley railway line in 1854, he built the Whitfield line to carry coal from the early Whitfield pits. Prior to the advent of steam, the railway wagons were hauled by horses. After Williamson died in 1867 many of his pits fell into decay and flooded. By 1848, Hugh's brother, Robert, had opened Goldendale Ironworks in the Chatterley Valley area of Tunstall, but by 1852 he had become less involved in the day-to-day management of the organisation and died in 1869. In the ensuing years Goldendale experienced a massive boom for its production of iron and could not extract sufficient coal from its mines to meet the demand of its blast furnaces. As a consequence, the Whitfield Colliery became part of the Chatterley organisation in 1872 and the railway network was expanded through a variety of branch lines to carry materials and men to and from the enterprises. This picture shows one of the Yorkshire Engine Company's 0-6-0 'Ogee' saddle-tank locomotives hauling a loaded coal train heading into Chatterley Whitfield on the private railway above the NSR Biddulph Valley line in the cutting below, c. 1928.

Opposite above: As the pottery firms sprang up and expanded so the town grew. Terraced housing was being built at an alarming rate in the late 1800s and early 1900s to keep pace with demand, many of the streets bearing the names of local employers or dignitaries of the day, e.g. Nash Peake Street, Williamson Street, Meir Street, Hawes Street, Dunning Street, etc. This picture shows a local builder clearing away stone rubble from a newly completed development as he contemplates the next phase.

Chatterley Whitfield had its own mineral line which ran from the colliery in the east to Pinnox Sidings at Brownhills on the outskirts of Tunstall. This train is carrying miners in converted vans which were once operated throughout Britain by the travelling American Circus of Messrs Barnum and Bailey. You can imagine the comments made about the passengers! However, they were a great improvement on the open wagons used to transport the miners prior to 1911. Each van was converted to hold 125 men.

In 1895, Walter Sylvester patented his invention of a ratcheted pulling device. For years the method of removing pit props in mines was to knock them out with a sledgehammer. Inevitably, this caused roof collapses which became the most common cause of fatality in the mines. Sylvester's invention enabled the removal of the pit props from a safe distance. A long chain would be attached to the prop and the other end secured to an immovable object. The chain was then tensioned by use of the ratchet and the pit prop was safely dislodged. Locally the device became known as a Walter, though nationally it was known as a Sylvester, and any miners still working up to the 1970s would have knowledge of this life-saving piece of equipment. This picture shows Sylvester's Scotia Works with the smoking bottle ovens of Henry Richards Tile Works in the background. By the 1930s Sylvester's had added motor car and lorry engineering to their vast range of general engineering skills.

The royal party leaves the factory. They later expressed their pleasure at what they had seen.

Opposite below: Alfred Meakin established his white earthenware manufactory at the Royal Albert Pottery in 1873. As the business expanded the Victoria and Highgate Potteries were added to the organisation. When the founder died in 1904, his son Alfred J. Meakin reconstructed the Highgate Pottery to accommodate the manufacture of glazed tiles. When he subsequently died, only four years later, in 1908, the Highgate Tile Works were purchased by Robert L. Johnson on behalf of his six sons. Soon after the Tile and Earthenware business separated to become Alfred Meakin (Tunstall) Ltd and H. & R. Johnson Ltd. Both organisations expanded and premises were rebuilt utilising the most modern machinery and equipment. By 1911, H. & R. Johnson's had developed into the largest tile manufacturer in Great Britain. Around the same time, Meakin's were developing the skills to produce ware decorated with the popular shade of blue known as Royal, or Mazarine Blue. Many manufacturers shied away from this colour because of the inconsistency of shade during firing. 'Blue de Roi' ware became a popular line in the Meakin's catalogue. This picture shows the decorated entrance to the pottery in anticipation of a visit from their majesties, King George V and Queen Mary, on Wednesday 23 April 1913. The following pages show the manufacturing processes and working conditions at the Meakin factories in 1913.

Modelling and mould making.

Making teacups by machinery.

48

The manufacture of vegetable dishes etc by hand.

Various articles being made by machine and stacked on boards prior to drying.

A similar workshop where plates are being made.

Oval dishes are manufactured here. Note how everyone is working by natural light alongside a window.

Finishing pottery prior to drying and then biscuit (bisque) firing.

The men in the foreground are filling saggars (fireclay containers) with ware, which are then placed inside the bottle ovens. Several men (placers) would be employed to stack the filled saggars around the inside of the oven as high as possible, whilst the kiln firemen prepared to carry out the firing process to generate temperatures in excess of 1,000 degrees centigrade.

These paintresses are applying the 'Blue de Roi' bands on the Biscuit Ware prior to glazing.

Some jobs were the sole occupations of women whilst others were done by men, but in the Dipping House men and women worked together.

An area where glazed ware is being placed in the saggars prior to loading in the Glost Oven.

In this decorating room the female workforce is applying the gold band to the 'Blue de Roi' ware. This occupation is known as gilding.

Above: Other girls and women are engaged in transferring patterns and designs to the ware.

Left: Once it is decorated, the ware is then placed into the Enamel Kiln for its final firing.

Opposite above: When the ware is fired and has cooled down it can be extracted from the ovens and sent to the warehouse for packing into orders.

Opposite below: In the packing department the ware is packed into crates, baskets or containers, depending on the size of the order, ready for despatch to the customer.

Left: This group of ten Enamel Kilns for the firing of coloured glazes on tiles was sited at the Highgate Tile Works.

Below: Because of the regular shape of the product, tile-making was able to be mechanised quite early on. Metal dies were forced upwards using a foot-operated treadle whilst a top die, controlled by a governed weight bore down from above and pressed the clay dust between the two to form the tile.

Above: Glazing could also be done by machinery.

Below: Female workers applied decoration to the tiles by hand.

Tiles are stacked into saggars ready to be fired.

In the spacious Glost Warehouse, tiles are being prepared for packing.

This aerial view gives a clear view of H. & R. Johnson's Highgate Tile Works. At the top right is Pinnox Street heading down towards Scotia Road. To the right of this road lies the Enoch Wedgwood & Co. factory with its six bottle ovens in a neat row. To the extreme top right of the picture is the Brownhills Tile Works which belonged to Richards Tiles Ltd.

Another image of tile makers at H. & R. Johnson.

In the Biscuit Warehouse tens of thousands of tiles were sorted and despatched to various Dipping Houses or Decorating Shops. The introduction of banks of rollers helped to take some of the heavy lifting from the job.

The advancement from bottle oven to continuous tunnel kilns had a huge impact on the environment. No more thick black smoke and soot billowing around the town and city. Again, the regular shape of the tile led to introduction of special stands, called 'cranks', which enabled maximum use to be made of the space on the kiln trucks.

Once the tiles had emerged from the other end of the kiln, after approximately twenty-four hours firing, they would be unloaded and sent to the Glost Warehouse for sorting and packing.

H. & R. Johnson were proud to have their own fleet of lorries which were used for a variety of purposes, including the despatch of the finished product to the customers premises.

This view of the Richards Tiles' Pinnox factory in Woodland Street is dated 1936. The factory occupies a large site which borders Woodland Street to the left, Williamson Street to the right and Scotia Road to the top. In later years the factory expanded towards the High Street (bottom of the picture) and, since its demise in the 1980s, the site is now completely occupied by a new ASDA store.

This was Richards Tile's flagship factory in 1936, the Brownhills Works, situated on Brownhills Road, adjacent to the Enoch Wedgwood factory and across the road from the H. & R. Johnson's Highgate Tile Works. The following images were all taken in 1936 on Richards Tiles' factories.

This picture shows the tile makers at work. The tiles are pressed and the surplus materials removed. The tiles are then stacked on bats on their way to biscuit firing.

One of the complementary products produced by Richards' was the 'Recesso' range of bathroom fittings. Unlike the production of tiles these items were cast in the traditional way using liquid clay, or 'slip' as it is known and would be decorated to match the colour range of tiles.

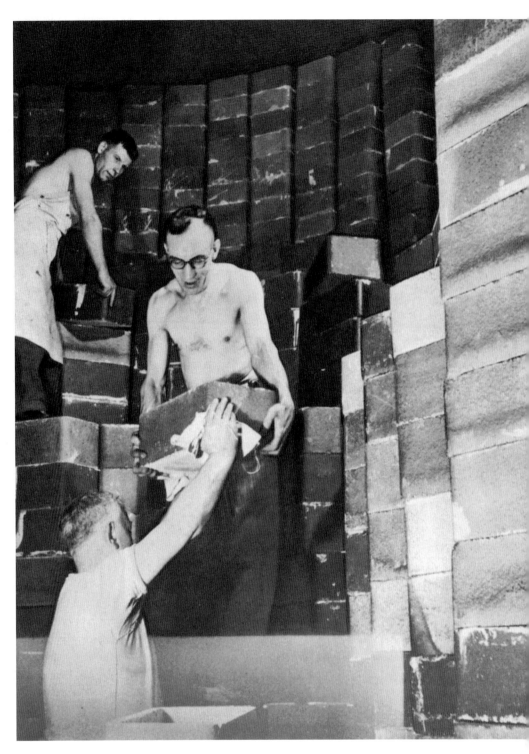

This picture shows the method of filling a bottle oven.

Right: Another range of products in the Richards' catalogue involved the production of mosaics. Tiles would be broken to shape and size using a hand-operated mechanical chisel. Often, patterns would be drawn onto a material backing-cloth and the tiles laid on the top. These 'sections' could then be pieced together like a jigsaw, laid in place, secured and grouted. This method saved a lot of time and effort.

Below: Richards' continuous tunnel kiln looks quite modern in this 1936 picture. The scene was still very similar in the 1970s and 80s, the main difference being the discontinuance of saggars to contain the ware. Kiln trucks were shunted around on miniature railway tracks to get them into position and the correct sequence for firing.

Above: Glost selectors stand in rows checking the fired ware for faults. A minor fault might render the product a 'seconds' to be sold at a lower price, but more obvious faults would cause the piece to be scrapped or recycled, and this was known as a 'pitcher'.

Left: Like other tile manufacturers, Richards Tiles also made fireplaces. These became popular in the 1950s and still exist in some homes today. The tile 'slabbers' job was very skilled. He had to build the fireplace inside out! The tiles would be laid face down in a pre-arranged pattern and secured in place. A filler would be added to create the 'slab'.

Here the fireplace maker is finishing off the article in preparation for fitting *in situ*. A builder would be able to fix the fireplace to the wall, attach a tiled hearth and fit the firebricks and linings ready to take a fire.

Stoke-on-Trent civic coat of arms is immortalised in this Richards Tile's mosaic.

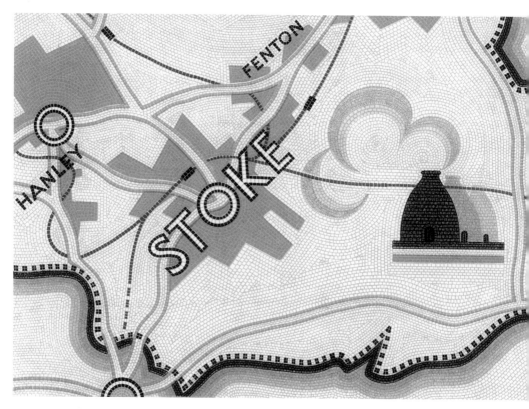

Many of the older generation from Stoke-on-Trent will remember Lewis's Arcade in Stafford Street, Hanley. It was memorable for several reasons. Some may recall that it contained a dance hall; some might recall that Lewis's Food Hall could be accessed from the arcade; others that it had a Travel Agent's shop whose window display consisted of (rarely seen) samples of foreign currency scattered about; some may recall that there was a record shop where (for the first time) you could listen to new releases via a set of headphones – Sherwin's went one better and had individual booths for their sampling opportunities – but the one thing that everyone will surely recall is the mosaic map of the Six Towns on the arcade floor! Here is a section of that mosaic proudly displayed in a Richards Tile's catalogue and sample guide.

five

Rest ...

'Work hard and play hard' is a very old maxim and quite appropriate to Tunstall folk.

In the late part of the nineteenth and early part of the twentieth centuries work was plentiful. The town was growing and thriving thanks to the potbanks and the mines. These major industries helped to create other peripheral, and equally essential, trades and business. Hauliers were needed to bring the coal, clay and other materials for the manufacture of pottery and other goods; engineering firms sprang up to provide necessary services such as die-making, tool-cutting, general maintenance etc; crate makers made containers for shipping the pottery wares; firms made the glazes and colours; and others supplied transfers and lithographs for the decoration of the ware... and so on.

Whole families could work at the same factory and relative wealth was created. Each town in the district became an autonomous place – despite Federation in 1910 and the amalgamation of the Six Towns into a city in 1925. All shopping needs could be catered for in the town so there was no need to travel far and wide.

Similarly, leisure facilities were also catered for in the locality. There were parks; football teams; Brownies, Guides, Cubs and Scouts; cinemas; billiard halls and the larger churches provided facilities for amateur dramatics and operatics. There were choirs and bands; and street parties were hastily arranged whenever a sufficiently important occasion arose. People generally enjoyed their leisure time and could do as little, or as much as their personal preferences demanded.

In a backyard in Copley Street, *c.* 1910. Tom Deakin's father and his three brothers are playing a game of skittles with their father. An upturned dolly-tub comes in very useful (but don't tell grandma or else there will be trouble!)

Right: In the 1920s charabanc outings were all the rage. Cooke Robinson's operated their successful depot from Phoenix Street. Here is charabanc No. 35, named Princess, ready for an outing. Wherever they're off to, seaside or countryside, they are guaranteed a good time with musical accompaniment thrown in for good measure.

Below: There was plenty of opportunity in the early part of the last century for a game of football and local teams were everywhere, competing against each other in the leagues and cup competitions. Any lad with talent could easily aspire to either of the two local teams, Stoke City or Port Vale, as they both consisted of local, home-grown talent in those days.

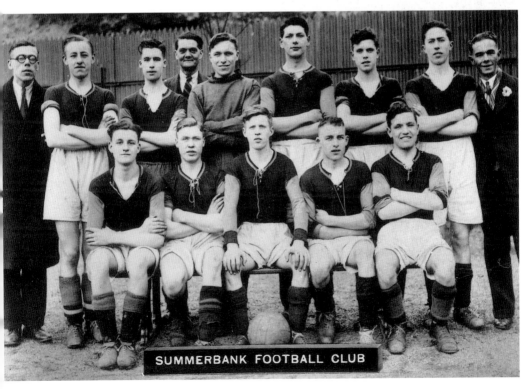

SUMMERBANK FOOTBALL CLUB

Apart from the school and church teams, Tunstall had its own town team. This picture shows the 1929/30 team.

Many of the larger pottery firms were quite paternalistic in their dealings with the workforce, particularly towards the children of the employees. For example, it was not unusual for the firms to organise Christmas parties and outings for them. Certainly altruistic on the one hand but, taking a cynical view, the firms were also keeping the next generation of workers happy and paving the way for their future employment at the works. This picture shows a Christmas party in the canteen at the factory of Enoch Wedgwood & Co. in the early 1950s. Elaine Evans (now Sutton), is enjoying a slap-up feast with her friends.

Street processions from the various churches in Tunstall were a familiar sight around the town right up to the early 1960s. The many anniversaries would be celebrated by a large turnout of parishioners, together with representatives of the many organisations associated with the life of each church. Here is a picture of the St Aidan's Brownies playing their part in a procession.

This children's party is taking place on the lawns of Greber House, which was previously the Presbytery to St Mary's Catholic church in Sun Street, (now St Aiden's Street). After Fr Ryan opened the Sacred Heart church in Queens Avenue in 1930 and subsequently built a new Presbytery, the old buildings were

sold to Mr Taylor who moved into the house and converted the church into a garage. The party on the lawn is to celebrate his daughter Christine's birthday

POTTERIES AND DISTRICT AMATEUR OPERATIC AND DRAMATIC SOCIETY.

Formerly Tunstall Amateur Operatic Society.

PRESENT

"GIPSY LOVE"

IN THE

QUEEN'S HALL BURSLEM

STOKE-ON-TRENT.

SEASON 1933.

SOUVENIR PROGRAMME.

JAMES HEAP (Hanley 1925) Ltd., Printers, Hanley.

The characters in this scene are Jonel (played by John Leak), Ilona (Ada M. Robinson, Joszi (Michael Gilligan), Julesa (Elsie Walmsley) and Jolan (Gertie Boulton).

Opposite: By 1933, the Tunstall Amateur Operatic Society (founded in 1926), had expanded to become the Potteries and District Amateur Operatic and Dramatic Society and on 16 October of that year they staged a six-night run of Franz Lehar's *Gipsy Love*.

Here we see Harry Dean, Cecil Kelsall and Gertie Boulton, playing the rôles of Kajetan, Dimitreanu and Jolan respectively.

One of the greatest regrets of many of the present-day visitors to Tunstall Park is the demise of the Conservatory which was part of the Floral Hall. Generations of people can recall the colourful displays of exotic flowers in bloom throughout the year. The Floral Hall was a popular venue for wedding receptions but sadly, these came to a stop in the 1990s when the whole building fell into disrepair. The Conservatory was demolished, leaving the concrete base and a bare wall as the only evidence of its previous existence.

Bond Street residents loved a party and made sure that whenever a special occasion arose the tables and chairs were brought out and the bunting raised. The parties were mainly for the children but in this picture we see the adults having their turn by celebrating VJ Day at the Bleeding Wolf pub in Scholar Green.

VE Day (8 May 1945) was celebrated in Bond Street with a huge party.

Everyone had chance to get in the picture, and Mr George Barber, owner of the Picture Palaces, offered a prize for the best decorated street. Not surprisingly Bond Street won. Local shopkeepers donated prizes for the children's competitions and races.

The Coronation of Queen Elizabeth II in 1953 brought another excuse for a street party. The flags were hoisted across the street, between the houses and once again the tables and chairs came out as everyone joined in the celebrations.

It looks as though each end of the street held their own celebrations.

The ladies seen here leaving a Bright Hour meeting at Wesley Place in around 1960, are (from left to right) Rosa Forster, Mrs Glanville (minister's wife), Mrs Capey (mother of Dora Capey), Mrs Alice Kerrigan, Mrs Ethel Barratt (mother of Brenda Bailey) and Mrs Lily Ebrill.

Brenda Barrett (now Bailey) makes a floral presentation. to Mrs Meir at the Autumn Fair, watched by
Mrs Johnson and Marjorie Windsor, c. 1934.

Tunstall WVS Darby and Joan Club in the 1950s. In the centre, at the back, are Mrs S.A. Deakin and
Mrs Minnie Brookes. Mrs Annie Longson Barker is on the extreme right, but who are the others?

This is one of the Darby and Joan Club's Christmas parties held at Tunstall Town Hall recorded in the early 1960s. Mrs Brookes is again on this photograph at the extreme left of the back row with Mrs Maria Tilstone in front.

Tunstall churches often staged pantomimes. They would be performed at the King Street (later Madison Street) Institute or the Jubilee Methodist church and were eagerly looked forward to by cast and audience alike. Here is the cast photograph from a 1948 performance of *Dick Whittington*.

Here is the whole cast pictured at the finale of the 1948 *Dick Whittington* pantomime.

In the February 1950 performance of *Babes in the Wood*, the babes were played by Christine Davies and Barbara Andrews; the Prince was played (in true pantomime tradition) by a female, in this case, Jenny Bossons. Brenda Maxfield played Maid Marion and Marion Jones was the Fairy Queen. Sarah was played by Margaret Chadwick and the Baron by Percy Atkins. Stan Davies played the cook and George Beswick played Henry. The robbers were played by Bill Davies and Norman Hancock. The cast was 'ably assisted' by Pat Shipley, Terry Jones and Tony Hancock, and the soloist in 'Alice Blue Gown' was Audrey Heath. In addition there was a chorus of forty-four and the production ran for two weeks!

Jubilee Methodist church (Gold Company) held their first pantomime in January 1951 and, some weeks later, a party was held in the Sunday School room to celebrate the successful production. In the foreground, left to right, are: Tom Rhodes, Cassie Rhodes (née Stone) and Harry Stone (brother of Mrs Rhodes). Among the others are Gordon Holdcroft (pianist) and his wife, Mrs Garner and Harry Garner; Mr and Mrs Harold Barber, Eric Brereton and Harry Dean (cast), Miss Joan Phillips (scenery), Nora Whalley, Mildred Poole, William Evans and Maurice Jones (cast), Richard Leigh (producer), Tom Deakin (electrics) and Mrs Leigh.

King Street Institute performed their production of Robinson Crusoe from 6 to 20 January 1951. The twelve babies shown here were played by Ann Barlow, Sylvia Copeland, Ann Windsor, Glenis Gidman, Barbara Shaw, Joan Hall, Christine Harratt, Valerie Hall, Betty Jane Webb, Linda Brough, Rosemary Johnson and Margaret Green.

Robinson Crusoe was played by Marion Jones, Polly Perkins by Brenda Maxfield, Jenny Green by Mavis Cooper, Ophelia Winterbottom by Jenny Bossons, Mrs Crusoe by Bill Davies, Ebeneza Trouble by Len Foxley, Man Friday by Tony Hancock, Will Atkins by Herbert Tilstone and Simple Simon by Norman Hancock. The principal dancers were Brenda Millward and Joyce Woodcock.

In the chorus were Rosa Dawson, Pat Shipley, Christine Heath, Cynthia Toft, Betty Plant, Joyce Wootton, Christine Horn, Barbara Twemlow, Brenda Jones, Beryl Hopkins, Sheila Ainsworth, June Wilshaw, May Cumberlidge, Vera Gilbert, Irene Harrop, Marie Ford, Sheila Harratt, Elaine Yates, Margaret Rhodes, Pauline Yates, Margaret Chadwick, Glenis Clutton and Doris Harrop.

By 1954, the King Street Institute had been renamed the Madison Street Institute, following the changing of several street names in Tunstall and beyond by the City Council. From 25 January to 6 February of that year, the Institute performed *Aladdin* with Jenny Pickerill playing the lead part; Widow Twankey was played by Norman Hancock; the Princess by Audrey Heath; Poo Puff by Tom Darlington; Floo Fluff by Betty Jones; the Fairy Queen by Marion Rowley; the Emperor by Len Foxley; Ting Ling by Eileen Yates; Abanezer by Maurice Jones; the Vizier by Derek Stubbs and the Genie of the Lamp by Arthur Machin.

In December of the same year, the players were back again performing another pantomime, *Dick Whittington*, which ran from 13 to 18 of the month. The commitment of the cast was phenomenal and the dedication of the other members who provided the direction, painted the scenery, played the music, made the costumes, applied the make-up and generally put the whole thing together was to be greatly admired. The lead was taken by Marion Rowley.

Above: The pantomime for 1957 was *The Prince and the Sea-Shell* by N.J. Hancock, and produced by S. Davies. The main roles were played by Eileen Yates, Valerie Beech, Mavis Cooper, Marion Rowley, Tom Darlington, Bill Davies, Norman Hancock and Len Foxley, with Judy Gallimore, R. Cheadle and C. Rigby.

The proceeds of this 1957 production were to be donated to the Christ Church and St Aidan's Restoration Funds.

Opposite below: Everyone enjoyed these performances and they were great occasions for bringing the congregation together. With the number of parts to be played and other numerous duties to be fulfilled there was something for everyone, whatever their talent.

George Barber was famous for his Picture Palace in The Boulevard (previously Station Road), but he also built the Regent Picture Palace in Hose Street off The Haymarket. This was a very popular venue for young and old alike, but in the 1960s it took on a new mantle. After it closed as a cinema it was refurbished and became The Golden Torch dance hall. It became famous amongst the younger generation as the home of Northern Soul and is still remembered with fondness by many for providing a touch of glamour in the town. Sadly, it no longer exists but there is still a cult following for Northern Soul and it is nostalgically referred to in the music history books.

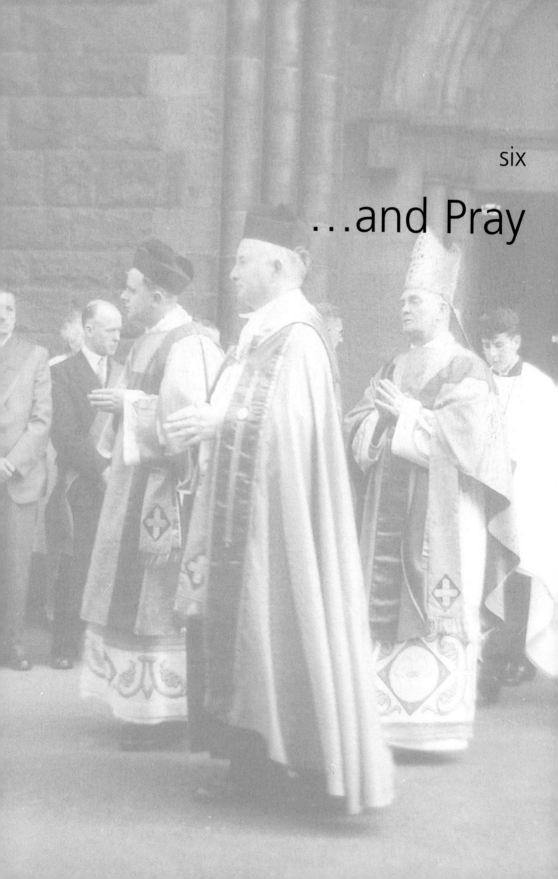

six

...and Pray

Present P.M. Chapel at Tunstall.

KING STREET WESLEYAN CHURCH.

Above: The Primitive Methodist Connexion built its first chapel, in Tunstall, in 1811, on the corner of Cross Street and Wellington Street, but the movement considered itself to have been founded in 1810. Consequently, its Jubilee was celebrated in 1860 and to commemorate it the old chapel was rebuilt and thus became the Primitive Methodist Jubilee Chapel. It was completed in time for the Jubilee Conference which was held in that year and was a grand edifice, often called the Cathedral of Primitive Methodism. It seated 1,500 and, over many years, gave wonderful service to the town and surrounding district. This picture shows the Jubilee Chapel after its refurbishment in 1905. It finally closed its doors in July 1971, after which it was demolished to make way for a large-scale redevelopment of the town. A few years earlier, the congregation had been joined by its Wesley Place neighbours and now the whole congregation was moving to King Street for a short period before the final move to a new purpose-built Methodist Church in Queens Avenue.

Left: King Street Wesleyan Methodist church was opened on 19 January 1875, having taken some fifteen months to build. It had seating for 700 and closed in 1975 prior to the move to Queens Avenue.

Sandyford Wesleyan church was built in 1910 on Cartlich Street.

Sandyford Wesleyan church interior with seating for a congregation of 200.

MOW COP, STAND 4, MONDAY AFTERNOON

This picture postcard of a Primitive Methodist Camp Meeting in 1910 is captioned: 'Mow Cop – Stand 4 – Monday Afternoon'. This meeting is very significant because it is celebrating the centenary of Primitive Methodism. The event was well-documented in a centenary publication which is why we can pinpoint this picture exactly. The precise date was Monday 20 June 1910 and the meeting took place from 2.30 p.m. to 4.00 p.m. There is a huge congregation milling around the speakers, who were Revd W. Tingle, Revd A. Jubb, and Revd J. Wellings. Stand 4 was manned by Mr J. Sivil, Mr M. Bourne, Mr G. Myers, Revd E. Dalton and Mr F. Knox. The presenter was Mr F. J. Bossons.

Opposite above: St Chad's Mission church was opened in King William Street in 1906. After its closure it lay empty for over twenty years before finally being demolished in 2004.

Opposite below: This is the reverse of the picture postcard asking recipients to send money. It states that the people (of the area) are entirely artisan in character, chiefly potters, colliers and iron-workers, and they have done their best to help themselves. Please help them! It's not entirely clear which mission church is being referred to since two opened around the same time: St Chad's, in King William Street and St Aidan's, in Summerbank Road. Perhaps the result of the appeal was so good the church was able to fund both missions.

NEW·MISSION·SCHOOL·CHURCH;·St CHAD'S·TUNSTALL.

DONATIONS will be
gratefully received by
Rev. D. W. Marsh,
St. Chad's House,
Tunstall, Staffs.

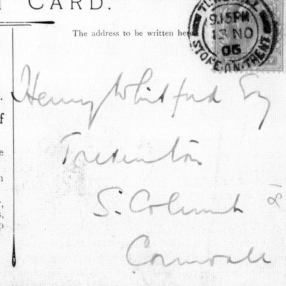

POST CARD.

This space may be used for correspondence.
(Post Office Regulation.)

The address to be written here

"A Cry from the Potteries."

CHRIST CHURCH, Tunstall, Staffs.

**New Mission Church Scheme for District of
4,000 people.   £500 urgently needed.**

Will you please send a small offering for the
Foundation Stone Laying.

An account of our work appeared in the "Church
Times" of Nov. 9th, 1906.

The people are entirely artizan in character,
chiefly potters, colliers, and iron-workers,
and they have done their best to help
themselves. **Please help them!**

Rev. J. A. NASH,
12, King Street,
TUNSTALL, Staffs.

This Picture shews Men of the Mission levelling the Site
of the New Church.

Henry Whitford Esq
Trenton
S. Columb
Cornwall

A dozen men, watched by twice as many children, have taken up their shovels ready to start work on the foundations of a new church. Christ Church issued this postcard to raise funds for the new Development Appeal in 1906.

This view of Christ Church was taken from Furlong Road. Christ Church was built in 1831/2 at a cost of £4,000. Extensions, designed by A.R. Wood were added in 1885/6.

Members of the Salvation Army make their way to their Corps HQ in Ladywell Road. via Wesley Place. The premises were built in 1863, initially as the Prince of Wales Theatre, later known as the Theatre Royal and also as St. James's Hall. The Hall closed circa 1880. The Salvation Army took over the building in 1882 and remained there until new purpose-built premises were built in Dunning Street a few years ago.

Above: The Salvation Army Songsters are seen here in Beckton Avenue on one of their processions.

Left: The Poulston family are seen here, *c.* 1920. All are resplendent in their uniforms, especially the young boy who was a budding junior bandsman.

This picture shows the junior bandsmen, *c.* 1955.

Above: The Salvation Army band poses happily for a formal photograph, 1950s.

Left: This is Captain Herbert Reeve, who was introduced as the commanding officer of the newly-formed Kidsgrove Corps of the Salvation Army in 1931. Did he have any involvement with the Tunstall Corps?

Right: St Aidan's Mission church, on Summerbank Road was built as a Chapel of Ease to Christ Church in 1907. This photograph was taken around 1937 and we see Pop Evans, Frank Powell, Bill Alcock and Les Bowcock.

Below: A view of the interior of St Aidan's from the baptistry.

Like the other churches in Tunstall, St Aidan's also had its processions. This one is making its way along Mount Street (now Knight Street), with Platt's butcher's shop and abattoir in the background.

Heading this St Aidan's Festival Walk are (from left to right), Frank Davies, Revd Howes and N. Hulme. Behind them are Mrs S. Davies in the centre and Mrs J. Woodcock on the right.

St Aidan's choir is pictured here in 1951.

Here is Sacred Heart Roman Catholic's 1948/49 Championship team. Back row, left to right: Fr Rohan, M. Mulroy, H. Jones, B. Quinn, T. Tynan, J. Bromley, M. McGreevey, J. McIver, T. Chadwick, T. Gilligan, R. Fradley, ? Turner, F. Murphy, B. Wood, M. Gilligan. Front row: G. Owen, J. Wilkes, J. Stanier, A. Stirk, T. Larvin, F. Gilligan, A. Dale, J. Farrell.

Another Sacred Heart Championship side from the late 1940s. Back row, left to right: Bernard Green, -?-, Sam Jones, Trevor Chadwick, Peter Jones, Bernard McLoughlan, Jimmy McDonald, Ken Brown, John Stanier, Terence Tynan, Bill Brown. Front row: Jack Barnett, Frank Smithson, Tommy Hancock, Arthur Stanyer, ? Turnock.

This is another Championship side photograph of the late 1940s.

Right: After the death of Fr Ryan, in 1951, the parishioners of Sacred Heart parish erected a magnificent crucifix memorial in Tunstall Cemetery in memory of his ministry to generations of families in the town. Sadly though, the memorial was vandalised beyond repair in 1993 after intruders had got into the cemetery one night and thrown rocks at it which smashed the figure of Christ into several pieces. The cross itself was also damaged, and it was decided that a replacement should be obtained as soon as possible. .Money was raised by parishioners and donations came from far and wide once people heard of this awful desecration. The new memorial, though smaller, is equally magnificent, and once more marks Fr Ryan's presence in the place where he bade farewell to so many of his parishioners over more than fifty years of his ministry. Members of the local Catholic firm of C. McGough and Sons, Funeral Directors, arranged for the stone and marble to be obtained from Italy and a local firm of memorial stone masons offered to erect the new memorial free of charge which concluded a wonderful collective effort by the people of Tunstall.

Below: A close-up view of the damage.

Left: The original memorial *in situ* shortly after its erection in the 1950s.

Below: This interior view of the Sacred Heart Catholic church was taken soon after it opened in 1930. All of the furnishings and the altar rails are in place. At this time the Mass was in Latin and the priest celebrated at the High Altar, with his back to the congregation. After Vatican II the rails were removed and are now in place in front of the side altars. At the same time the sanctuary area was extended and brought forward towards the congregation and a new altar was erected close to the front and facing the people. From this point the Mass was celebrated in English.

Fr Tom Rohan was curate at Tunstall from 1947 to 1952. Here he is pictured with Bishop Humphrey Bright leading a trip to Cotton College. Among the young parishioners who went on the trip are Wendy Mulroy, Sheila Cooper (now Broad), Terry Tynan, Maureen Curran, Beryl Fletcher, John Stanier, Kathleen Cartwright, Michael McGreavey, George Guest, Tony McGreavey, Michael Mulroy, Peter Jones and Ann McGough.

Another Catholic procession makes its way through the town in the late 1950s. Bishop Bright appears to be in good voice as he sets the pace.

More members of the Legion of Mary join the procession. At the extreme right of the picture, in the dark coats, are Marie Cole and her mother.

Opposite above: Banners are assembled outside the west doors of the Sacred Heart church ready to join a procession. Pictured, from left to right, are: –?–, Mr O'Grady, Harold Jones, Jim Farrell, Mick Looskin, Frank Butler, –?–, Frank Loftus.

Opposite below: This 1950s procession shows some of the Sacred Heart ladies walking from the High Street into the Haymarket. Amongst them are Mrs Mulroy and Ada Ward.

A procession leaves the Sacred Heart church in the 1950s. Bishop Bright is resplendent in his formal vestments.

Opposite above: This is the Sacred Heart choir, *c.* 1949/50. Back row, left to right: Mary Loftus, Kath Brown, Kath Mulroy, Alf Stirk, Sheila Walker, Fr Ryan, Kath Minshall, Joe Waters, Chris Boulton, Gertie Wareham, Fr Rohan, Kath Jordan, Eileen Baillie, ? Stirk. Front row: -?-, Jean Birtles, Monica Hancock, Mick Gilligan (choirmaster), Dick Stanworth (organist), Mary Ford, Winnie Quinn, Winnie McGreavey.

Opposite below: Priests and Altar Servers who were present at the Opening Mass of the new Sacred Heart Catholic Church in June 1930. Back row, left to right: Lawrence Nixon, Wilfred Morris, Wilfred Dillon, Jim Williams, Tom Longshaw, Victor Holland. Middle row: Philip Williams, Frank Quinn, Myles McGough, Sam Manifold, Revd P. J. Ryan, Revd J. McDonald, Tom Ainsworth, Martin Kane. Front row: Jack McGough, Joe McGough, George Bell, Lawrence McMinn, Bernard McGreavey, Fred McGough, Clement Dillon, Albert Woolrich, Eddie Nixon.

An aerial view of Tunstall, taken around 1960, showing clearly the large copper-covered domes of the Sacred Heart church on Queens Avenue to the left of centre. The large portion of the lower picture is taken up by the park, and running across the picture to the top side of the park is Victoria Park Road leading towards King William Street to the left. Note that Victoria Park Road is a continuous route into The Boulevard and traffic travelling along Queens Avenue and up King William Street is obliged to stop and give way. Today, Queens Avenue has the priority of the continuous route and traffic stops at the end of Victoria Park Road. Behind the houses on King William Street can be seen Tunstall railway station and the lines running behind the houses on Victoria Park Road towards Pittshill. Beyond the station at the top left of the picture is the Alexandra Pottery works of Johnson Bros. This has recently been demolished and the land is awaiting development. At the top right of the picture can be seen the Memorial Park on The Boulevard, across from which is Barber's Picture Palace. Above the cinema lies the Soho Mills. This property was soon to be demolished to make way for new traffic improvements and the extension of Scotia Road.

seven

People

Left: John Baskeyfield is shown here as Chief Bailiff of Tunstall in 1900 and 1901. This position was created in 1855, when the first Chief Bailiff was Mr Enoch Wedgwood. Tunstall Urban District Council was formed in 1895 and the Chairman of the UDC retained the title of Chief Bailiff for some years after. The position disappeared completely in 1910 when the Federation of the Six Towns took place. During his term of office, in 1896-97, W. Boulton presented a chain of office to commemorate the Diamond Jubilee.

Below: A long-service presentation to members of Wesley Place choir. From left to right: Alice Sutton, Tom Naylor, Mary Naylor, Ethel Barratt and Will Cook.

This photograph was taken in September 1886 at Glen Helen on the Isle of Man. Standing, from left to right, are Enoch Bennett, solicitor and father of Arnold Bennett, the Potteries author; Arthur Wilkinson, Absolom Reade Wood, architect and Town Surveyor of Tunstall; John Beardmore, solicitor. Seated to the left is Tom Bennett, of Dunn, Bennett & Co. and, on the right, is Thomas Francis Wood, father of Harry Wood, of Wood & Sons. A.R. Wood became a prolific architect and is responsible for the design of many of the public buildings, churches and schools in Tunstall and beyond. His legacy lives on and Wood, Goldstraw, Yorath are still in existence today and hold an important place in the design of public architecture, especially schools and churches, in the city and beyond.

Willie Windsor sells a *Sentinel* to his sister Ethel Barrett in Princess Street, Tunstall, *c.* 1948. Willie was disabled from birth but earned his living by selling daily papers and the *Sentinel* around the town for over fifty years.

This group from of ladies from the Women's Section of Tunstall Labour Party (and their husbands) are visiting their Member of Parliament at Westminster just after the Second World War. It is possible to see shell damage on the walls of the building behind the group. The MP was Albert Edward Davies and he is to be found in the centre of the group (bespectacled) behind the lady in the pale coloured coat. Mr Davies was born in 1900 and raised in Smallthorne as a member of the Methodist Church. He held strong political views for which he was respected by his peers and he held many offices in and out of parliament. Sadly, in 1953 he died after he was taken ill on board ship on his way to the West Indies as a member of a parliamentary delegation. He was survived by his wife and son, James Edward. Also in the picture are (second from right) Ethel Barratt; (fourth from right) Brenda Barratt (now Bailey); (fifth from right) Flo Jones. Walter McIntyre is the tall man at the back next to Albert Davies.

Here are the Summerbank ARP Wardens in the Second World War. Among the men can be found, back row, left to right: ? Bailey, S. Davies, ? Woollam, R. Stirk, A. Taylor, L. Washington. Middle row: ? Wooollam, ? Evans, ? Crompton. Front Row: J. Holmes, ? Johnson, E. Austin, A. Greatbach. Can anyone complete the list?

During the twentieth century, Tunstall has been honoured to provide several Lord Mayors to the City of Stoke-on-Trent, all of whom were well-known, prominent people in the town and had strong Methodist connections. The first was George Herbert Barber in 1929-30 (see chapter on Station Road).

Alderman G. Leonard Barber (grandson of Ald. G.H. Barber) served as Lord Mayor. in 1952-53.

Alderman Annie Longson Barker followed in
1954-55.

Alderman Harold Naylor was Lord Mayor in
1955-56.

Alderman and Mrs Barber are shown here attending a bazaar for the Haywood and Tunstall War Memorial Hospital held at the Town Hall in Tunstall during his year of office.

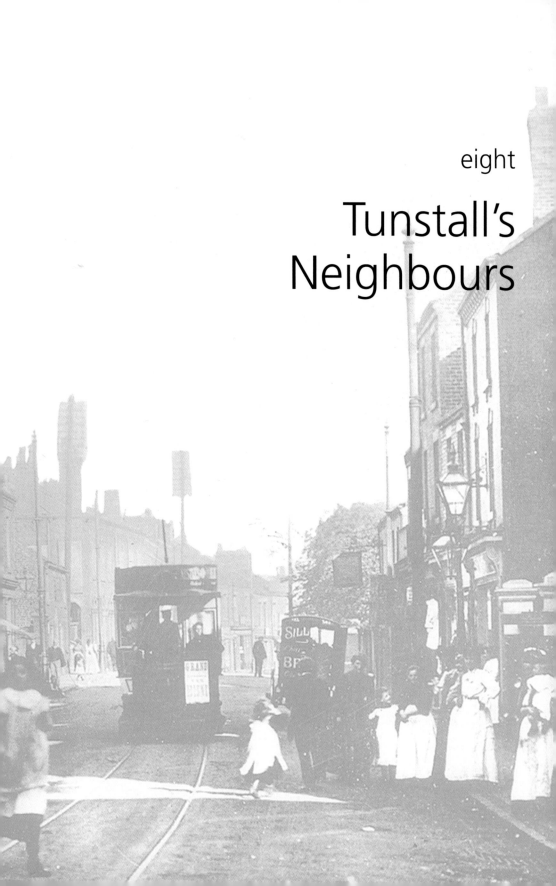

eight

Tunstall's Neighbours

An early view of Goldenhill showing a tram on its journey along the High Street. On the right of the picture, just beyond the tram, is Harry Sillito's delivery cart standing outside his grocery shop at No. 9 and next door, at No. 7, was the butcher's shop of George Holdings. Both of these businesses began trading in the late 1800s. By 1921, this little concentration of shops was occupied by Miss Annie Gibson, a milliner, at No. 1. Green & Ramsey Ltd, grocers, at No. 3 and Bickley Bros, drapers at No. 5. Sillito and Holdings still occupied Nos. 7 and 9 and then there was the post office and stationers at Nos. 11 and 13, run by Miss R.M. Lewis. Next to her, at No. 15 was John Neate's butcher's shop. Plenty of choice, and competition, for the people of Goldenhill.

At the far end of Goldenhill, in an area called Head o' th' Lane, at Oldcott Green, was Red Lion Square. This became the terminus for the trams which were operated by the Potteries Electric Traction Company between Hanley and Goldenhill in the period 1900 to 1928. This picture was taken around 1916. Motor buses were introduced from 1914 and had replaced the trams completely by 1928. The terminus then became the new bus depot.

Another view from 1916, just past Red Lion Square, shows Oldcott Green's row of terraced houses, and in the distance is the top of Kidsgrove Bank.

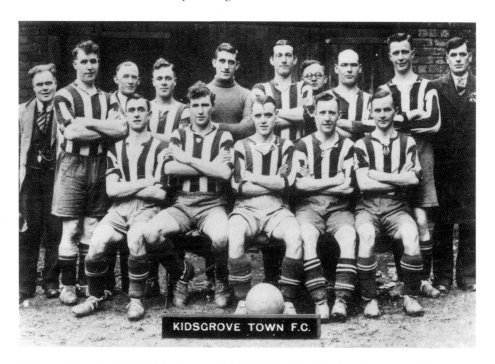

KIDSGROVE TOWN F.C.

Kidsgrove Town Football Club is a long-established local club which has always enjoyed success in the area and minor leagues.

The Revd John Francis Hewitt MA, Vicar of St James' parish church, Newchapel from 1910 to 1916 with choir and choirmaster, Mr Owen Mollart.

Harriseahead Prize Jazz Band had a terrific following. In this picture there are seventy smiling faces, of all ages. Surely this will bring back floods of memories?

Harriseahead School pupils obviously needed no excuse to dress up. There is one of everything here (and two or more of something!) in this wonderful picture from the 1920s. The costumes and makeup are magnificent and there seems to be more than one hidden message in there too.

St. Michaels Road, Pittshill, leading out of Tunstall and heading up towards Chell. This is often referred to as Pittshill Bank (which is really what it is) though the true Pittshill Bank still exists and is tucked away out of sight close to the junction with Furlong Road.

This lovely delivery cart belonged to F. Roberts and Sons, grocers and bakers, of Brindley Ford, whose business was operating in the 1920s.

An early 1900s photograph of another local football team, Brown Lees PSA.

Longport station was opened on 9 October 1848 on the main line of the North Staff's Railway. This picture was taken 104 years later, in 1952. Level crossing gates are still in operation in this view, though a footbridge was a later alternative addition.

A tram parks alongside its successor – the old and new. As we have seen, the Potteries Electric Traction Company operated trams between 1900 and 1928 when buses became fully operational. Here we see tram No. 82, a forty-seater, built in 1900-1 by the Midland Carriage and Wagon Company. It was sold to Wemyss and District Tramways in 1928 and ran until 1933. The bus, EH 7901 was one of two built in 1926 and bore the number 88. It operated between Goldenhill and Longton, travelling via Hanley and Stoke. Inevitably, it would have taken in Tunstall and Burslem also. The bus ran until 1935 and was disposed of to Lewis (Breakers) of Hanley.

Other local titles published by Tempus

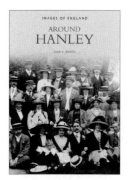

Around Hanley

JOHN BOOTH

This fascinating collection of photographs illustrates life as it was in and around the pottery town of Hanley. Originally just a single farm, Hanley grew into the largest and most central town in the greater area of Stoke-on-Trent, blossoming in the early twentieth century with the development of heavy industry. This pictorial history reflects the town as it was at that time, at the height of its success.

0 7524 3407 1

Around Stafford

ROY LEWIS

Containing more than 200 photographs, this fascinating collection examines the sweeping changes that have taken place in Stafford and the surrounding villages of Gnosall, Haughton and Sandon over the last century. The streets, buildings, schools, churches and factories (such as Lotus the shoe manufacturers and GEC, formerly English Electric) are illustrated alongside events such as the annual hospital pageant, village sports meetings, royal visits and other special occasions in the delightful tribute to the area.

0 7524 1811 4

Burton upon Trent Pubs

DAVID MOORE AND GRAHAM COXON

Illustrated with over 170 images, this pictorial history of the public houses of Burton upon Trent reveals how the town has developed and changed over the years. Pubs with strange names like the Hoop and Adze, the Old English Gentleman and the Who'd a Thought It are featured alongside town centre pubs and back street boozers, famous landlords, sports teams, mascots and of course customers in this journey into Burton's brewing history.

0 7524 3255 9

Tunstall

DON HENSHALL

Reference is made to Tunstall as early as 1086 but it was the growth of the pottery industry in the nineteenth century which transformed the village into a thriving town. This fascinating collection of over 180 archive photographs depicts the history of the town, exploring the people, places, industry and leisure of the area over the past 150 years. The result is a volume which will awaken nostalgic memories for many and will delight anyone interested in the history of the area.

0 7524 3721 6

If you are interested in purchasing other books published by Tempus, or in case you have difficulty finding any Tempus books in your local bookshop, you can also place orders directly through our website

www.tempus-publishing.com